Daly Sales Motivators

Timeless Sales Wisdom
From The Ages For The Ages

Daly Sales Motivators

Timeless Sales Wisdom
From The Ages For The Ages

366 Action Ideas To
GROW SALES
JACK DALY

PSCI Publishing
La Jolla, California

Daly Sales Motivators
Timeless Sales Wisdom from the Ages for the Ages
366 Action Ideas to Grow Sales

Jack Daly

Copyright © 2001 Jack Daly

Published by:
PSCI Publishing
5842 La Jolla Corona Drive
La Jolla, CA 92037

Phone: (888) 298-6868
Fax: (858) 454-5481
www.ProfessionalSalesCoach.net

Cover design and inside layout: Ad Graphics, Inc., Tulsa, OK
Printed in the United States of America

ISBN: 0-9712126-0-0

WHAT OTHERS ARE SAYING ABOUT JACK DALY...

"On behalf of *Inc. Magazine*, I would like to thank you for your participation. In our tenth annual growing the company conference . . . your session was evaluated by attendees based on a scale of 4 (excellent) to 1 (poor). The average of the scores given to you by the attendees is 3.96 . . . the highest scoring session!"

Beth Sheehan, Conference Producer
Inc. Magazine

"Words cannot adequately express my gratitude and appreciation for the tremendous presentation you gave at our national sales meeting. Your professionalism and enthusiastic delivery were one of the best we ever had. It is not often that our sales force awards a guest speaker with a standing ovation."

Jeff Muecke, VP Sales
Universal Technical Institute

"Thank you so much for your tremendous contribution to the Caribbean Cruise University! We received an abundance of positive feedback during the conference, and as usual, you were our highest rated speaker."

Heather E. Henderson, Program Director
Young Entrepreneurs Organization (YEO)

"I didn't need to tell you what it takes to hold the attention of an 'ALL-CEO' group such as mine, because you did it. All too often, speakers come from theory without practice. Your background indicated 'you've been there' and your presentation showed for it. The most frequent comment heard was the amount of immediately implementable action ideas delivered."

Dick Swanson, Chairman
The Executive Committee, (TEC)

"When I first heard Jack Daly speak at the national conference earlier this year, I just knew we had to bring him to Milwaukee. He takes powerful material, adds his personal street smarts and actual experience, and delivers a wallop of words that every CEO needs to hear once in a while. And I want my top sales person to hear the same message with me."

Peter Gottsacker, President
Wixon Fontarome

DEDICATED TO:

My son Adam, whose interpersonal charm and creativity provide infinite opportunities.

.

My daughter Melissa, whose focus and commitment to excellence are exceeded only by her niceness.

My wife Bonnie, whose self sacrifices and support are unending and too often taken for granted. Thanks from all of us.

Acknowledgments

To the many folks with more smarts and wit than me, from whom I've drawn quotes and sales axioms reflected here in this book and elsewhere in my life, a most grateful thanks.

A special thanks to Jim Pratt, a key mentor for me in business, professional speaking, and life.

Lastly, thanks to our "Directors of First Impressions" led by Caroline Hill at Platinum Capital Group, for their steady cheerfulness on the phones while laboring through the many typed versions of this collection.

INTRODUCTION

Here are insights into the real world of sales, in the fewest words. It's hoped that these timeless sales sayings inspire the readers to take action toward helping their customers be more successful.

Daily Sales Motivators

Timeless Sales Wisdom
From The Ages For The Ages

366 Action Ideas To
GROW SALES

#1 January 1

The future does not get better by hope; it gets better by plan, and to plan for the future we need goals.

Jim Rohn

#2 January 2

We cannot become what we need to be by remaining what we are.

Max De Pree

#3 January 3

Goals should be specific, realistic and measurable.

William G. Dyer

#4 January 4

You can and you should shape your own future, because if you don't, somebody else surely will.

Robert Barker

#5 January 5

The five essential entrepreneurial skills for success: concentration, discrimination, organization, innovation and communication.

Michael E. Gerber

#6 January 6

Manage your business to increase value, not sales.

Peter Collins

#7 January 7

Retail sales are very basic. Treat each client as if they were one of your grandparents and you will never make a mistake. Treat them well and they will be clients for life.

Barry Steinberg

#8 January 8

Most people buy not because they believe, but because the salesman believes.

Rick Jory

#9 January 9

You may be disappointed if you fail, but you are doomed if you don't try.

Beverly Sills

#10 January 10

It takes a lot of unspectacular preparation to produce spectacular results.

#11 January 11

The things that got you to where you are today are not the things that will get you to the future.

Peter Drucker

#12 January 12

Are you proactively expanding your business? Can you name your ten top prospects? Why are they hesitating to do business with you?

#13 January 13

Risk believing in yourself. Until you test the limits regarding what you can achieve, you can't truly know what your chances really are. The major obstacle to overcoming the odds is never challenging them.

#14 January 14

Do what you are expected to do, and you will survive. Do more than you are expected to do, and you will thrive.

#15 January 15

Better to be interested than to be interesting. Let the prospect take center stage.

#16 January 16

Where you are and where you want to be are two different places. To close the gap, you must change.

#17 January 17

If you really believe you can be, have, or do something, you will create the circumstances and find the people to allow you to be, have, or do.

#18 January 18

Two people who want to do business together won't let the details keep it from happening. If two people don't want to do business together, the details won't make it happen.

#19 January 19

Never be late—period.

#20 January 20

A man can succeed at almost anything for which he has unlimited enthusiasm.

Charles Schwab

#21 January 21

The quality and quantity of your relationships is directly tied to the amount of value you continually inject into them.

#22 January 22

The road to success is full of potholes. The key is to continue the journey.

#23 January 23

Make enthusiasm your daily habit.

#24 January 24

There's a big difference between selling and helping people to buy. Helping people to buy matches their needs with proper solutions. Selling creates a sale. Helping people to buy creates customers.

Michael LeBoeuf

#25 January 25

You're not learning anything when you're talking.

#26 January 26

Keep track of a week's work in one-hour segments, once each quarter. Adjust your schedule to ensure sales effectiveness.

#27 January 27

Motivation is what gets you started. Habit is what keeps you going.

Jim Ryan

#28 January 28

The short course to effective selling: Ask questions and listen.

#29 January 29

The most common characteristic of successful people is that they know where they are going. They are determined to reach their goals and won't let any obstacles discourage them.

#30 January 30

There is no such thing as a routine sales call.

#31 *January 31*

Each day, at some point, stop and ask yourself, "Is what I'm doing moving me toward my goals? Is it a priority?"

#32 *February 1*

The successful person knows precisely what she desires, has a plan for getting it, believes in her ability to get it, and devotes a major portion of her time to acquiring it.

#33 *February 2*

Great opportunities await those who give more than what is asked. I encourage you to put the uncommon touch on even the most common task. We may never have the opportunity to do great things in a great way, but we all have the chance to do small things in a great way.

#34 *February 3*

Promise only what you can deliver. Then deliver more than you promise.

#35 February 4

These traits should be modeled by any sales person wishing to attain higher levels of success.

1. They have **personal integrity/intellectual honesty**

2. They maintain a **sense of urgency/high motivation**

3. They have a high level of **responsibility/ follow through**

4. They **focus on results, not success or failures**

5. They are **motivated by rejection**

6. They are **relationship managers**

7. They are **visible and accessible**

8. They **play the productivity game**—quality vs. quantity

9. They are **confident and expect success**

10. They always **anchor performance with thank-you**

#36 February 5

Being physically fit is a pillar of the foundation of success. Physical fitness can't be stored. Fitness is the result of ongoing, concentrated aerobic activity along with proper dietary balance.

#37 February 6

Do you create sales opportunities or just react to them?

#38 February 7

Don't let your ego get in the way . . . anytime over anything.

#39 February 8

If you were your own competitor, how would you win over your account?

#40 February 9

Keep a "things to do" list and revise it every day. Crossing things off the list is very satisfying.

#41 February 10

We all have two choices: we can make a living or we can design a life.

#42 February 11

If you make a sale you make a living. If you make an investment of time and good service in a customer, you can make a fortune.

#43 February 12

The most important word in the English language, if you want to be a success, can't be found in the dictionary. It's rolodex.

Harvey Mackay

#44 February 13

Sales people who reach the highest levels of success regularly weed out a lot of clients. Don't be afraid to let go of marginal prospects because they are time-wasters.

#45 February 14

Have fun and celebrate your successes.

#46 February 15

It is easier to get forgiveness than permission.

#47 February 16

Selling is the easiest job in the world if you work it hard but the hardest job in the world if you try to work it easy.

#48 *February 17*

Somebody should tell us, right at the start of our lives, that we are dying. Then we might live life to the limit, every minute of every day. Do it! I say. Whatever you want to do, do it now! There are only so many tomorrows.

Michael Robbins

#49 *February 18*

The best way to brag about yourself is to let other people do it for you.

#50 *February 19*

If you look just like your competitors, expect to perform just like your competitors.

#51 *February 20*

Marketing is an attitude, not a department.

Phil Wexler

#52 *February 21*

Rarely is price the only deciding consideration. Dig deeper!

#53 February 22

Anyone too busy to say thank you will get fewer and fewer chances to say it.

#54 February 23

If it seems like you've got everything under control, you're just not going fast enough.

Mario Andretti

#55 February 24

Change is inevitable, growth is optional.

Jim Kenefick

#56 February 25

Either you run the day or the day runs you!

Jim Rohn

#57 February 26

If it's meant to be, it's up to me.

#58 February 27

What you do speaks so loudly that I cannot hear what you say.

Ralph Waldo Emerson

#59 February 28

My greatest strength as a consultant is to be ignorant and ask a few questions.

Peter Drucker

#60 February 29

The race is not always won by the fastest runner but sometimes by those who just keep running. Persistence Pays!

#61 March 1

Your professionalism is determined by the way you are in business, not by the business you are in.

#62 March 2

The more similar the services, the more important the differences.

Harry Beckwith

#63 March 3

No one will ever pay you what your product is worth. They will pay you what they think it is worth.

Chuck Reaves

#64 *March 4*

It is much harder to ask the right question than it is to find the wrong question.

E.E. Morison

#65 *March 5*

We are what we repeatedly do. Excellence, then, is not an act but a habit.

Aristotle

#66 *March 6*

Act like a consultant . . . because that's really what you are!

#67 *March 7*

It doesn't get any simpler than this: be the first in and the last out.

#68 *March 8*

A goal is a dream with a deadline.

Harvey Mackay

#69 March 9

You can observe a lot by just watching.

Yogi Berra

#70 March 10

If you don't have an assistant, you are one.

Ralph Roberts

#71 March 11

Success comes from doing what we know we should be doing, when we should be doing it, whether we want to or not. Self discipline!

#72 March 12

Under promise, over perform.

#73 March 13

People do things for their reasons not ours. Find out your prospect's wants.

#74 March 14

It isn't what you know that counts; it's what you do with what you know that counts.

#75 March 15

Do you want more business? See fewer people! Build relationships.

#76 March 16

Help your clients be more successful and no competition will ever take them away from you.

#77 March 17

No time management strategy will solve a self-discipline problem.

#78 March 18

No worthwhile effort is ever lost. Do the right thing, and the payback will be there.

#79 March 19

Looking for more energy? Maintain a regular exercise and diet program.

#80 March 20

The two greatest cures for call reluctance are knowledge and action.

#81 March 21

If you focus hard enough on why something won't work, chances are it won't. Avoid becoming the "abominable no-man."

#82 March 22

No one ever lost a sale by listening too closely.

Robert Epstein

#83 March 23

Failure to prepare is preparing to fail.

John Wooden

#84 March 24

Sales records are an absolute must—keep them, analyze them, learn from them.

#85 March 25

More sales are lost each year through neglect than for any other reason.

#86 March 26

Each evening write down the six most important things you have to do the next day. By deciding what's most important, you can follow what you set out to do and not go off on tangents.

#87 March 27

If you have nothing to say, say nothing. You'll get that much more attention when you do speak out.

#88 March 28

If you keep waiting for just the right time, you may never begin. Begin now! Begin where you are with what you are.

#89 March 29

When you start taking your customers for granted, you start losing them.

#90 March 30

Think share of customer instead of market share.

#91 March 31

If you consistently have to be the cheapest to get the order, you're not a professional salesperson.

#92 April 1

Professional persistence pays. Eighty percent of sales occur after the fifth call.

#93 April 2

Proactively growing your business entails consistently concentrating on building new business. You never know when or how you will lose one of your prized accounts.

#94 April 3

The customer's perception is reality.

#95 April 4

Know where your sales increases will come from. They won't just happen!

#96 April 5

Know how your products differ from those of your competitors.

#97 April 6

"Customers" do business with you occasionally; "Clients" provide an ongoing stream of business with you. Sales professionals strive for a "Clientele."

#98 April 7

At the end of each day you should play back the tapes of your performance. The results should either applaud you or prod you.

#99 April 8

I find it fascinating that most people plan their vacations with better care than they do their lives. Perhaps that is because escape is easier than change.

#100 April 9

The worst days of those who enjoy what they do are better than the best days of those who don't.

#101 April 10

Success is nothing more than a few simple disciplines, practiced every day, while failure is simply a few errors in judgement, repeated every day. It is the accumulative weight of our disciplines and our judgements that leads us to either fortune or failure.

#102 April 11

Selling is about the building of long-term relationships.

Bev Hyman

#103 April 12

Selling is motivational and not persuasion.

#104 April 13

I am convinced that life is 10 percent what happens to me and 90 percent how I react to it. And so it is with you . . . we are in charge of our attitudes.

Charles Swindoll

#105 April 14

Referrals are the lifeblood of a successful career in sales. And yet sales people are too often reluctant to ask for them. Ask for referrals!

#106 April 15

Price is not an objection but lack of perceived value.

#107 April 16

Update your voice mail message daily. Make it unique, informative and maybe even fun. Resist sameness: "your call is important . . . I'm either away . . . ." Boring!

#108 April 17

Every price is too high until they see the benefits.

#109 April 18

Be more concerned with your character than your reputation, because your character is what you really are, while your reputation is merely what others think you are.

#110 April 19

There's only one business to be in and it's called . . . capturing and keeping customers!

#111 April 20

It's not who you know, it's who knows you.

#112 April 21

Yard by yard, life is hard, but inch by inch, it's a cinch. (Every long-term plan should have short-term steps)

Robert Schuller

#113 April 22

You don't quit trying when you lose; you lose because you quit trying.

#114 April 23

You can't figure out what to do in the future by looking at how you did things in the past.

#115 April 24

Success seems to be largely a matter of hanging on after others have let go.

William Feather

#116 April 25

When products or services are perceived to be equal, people will buy from the company which is easier to do business with.

#117 April 26

Giving up is the ultimate tragedy.

Robert Donovan

#118 April 27

There's a lot more in each of us than any of us suspects. Undoubtedly many former athletes had the power to run the four-minute mile. It was a barrier only until one man achieved it!

Charles Rudman

#119 April 28

If you are going to lose your job, be sure it's for what you did . . . not for what you didn't do.

#120 April 29

Nothing is particularly hard if you divide it into small jobs.

#121 April 30

When a goal is well stated, it is always visually imaginable or exceptionally simple.

#122 May 1

It is ironic, but true, that in this age of electronic communications, personal interaction is becoming more important than ever.

Regis Mckenna

#123 May 2

Keep the right goal in mind: Don't look for money, look for applause. If you create something of value the sales will come.

Robert Ronstadt

#124 May 3

Live as if you were to die tomorrow. Learn as if you were to live forever.

Gandhi

#125 May 4

If you listen closely enough, your customers will explain your business to you.

Peter Schutz

#126 May 5

Blame no one, expect nothing, do something.

Curt Dyckman

#127 May 6

Having something to say is always more important than wanting to say something.

#128 May 7

The critical path to relationship selling involves 50% of our time identifying the need/opportunity/problem. This requires active listening.

#129 May 8

Whether you believe you can or believe you can't, you're right.

#130 May 9

If I had eight hours to chop down a tree, I'd spend six sharpening my axe.

Abraham Lincoln

#131 May 10

Don't spend time on anything your customers don't perceive to be of value.

Michael Basch

#132 May 11

More people would learn from their mistakes, if they weren't so busy denying them.

#133 May 12

He who ceases getting better, ceases being good. The true professional practices lifelong learning.

#134 May 13

Am I living on my own fat? Regularly upgrade your clients, and protect from "hardening of the arteries."

Jim Pratt

#135 May 14

Focus precedes success. Goal orientation is key—write them down.

#136 May 15

The person who listens is in command. Listening—is your professional duty.

#137 May 16

You are the message. It's not what you say but what you do.

#138 May 17

Relationships are targeted efforts, not random occurrences.

#139 May 18

Destiny is not a matter of chance; it is a matter of choice.

#140 May 19

A sales person who "shows up and throws up" should be sued for malpractice. Discover the needs of your prospects and clients.

#141 May 20

Hire an administrator and be your own sales manager. Don't allow paperwork to keep you from your clients.

#142 May 21

The harder you work the luckier you get.

#143 May 22

Unseen—Unheard—Unsold.

#144 May 23

A goal without a defined strategy to achieve . . . is not a goal.

#145 May 24

There is a difference between interest in, or knowledge of, and total passionate commitment.

#146 May 25

Solicit your customers regarding your performance. It's the only opinion that truly counts.

#147 May 26

Never skimp on distributing your business cards.

#148 May 27

Assemble a "Power Group" representing 10-12 top clients/prospects, for purposes of idea sharing and value add to their businesses.

#149 May 28

Concentrate on client development, not customer transactions.

#150 May 29

You can't score if you keep the bat on your shoulder.

#151 May 30

Proactive listening entails taking notes.

#152 May 31

Strive to be an "impact player," someone who makes a difference, with each of your clients.

#153 June 1

You've got to either paddle your canoe faster than the water or slower. You just can't let the water take you where it wants.

#154 June 2

Prescription without explanation is malpractice. Ask more questions!

#155 June 3

Whatever the mind of a man can conceive and believe, the mind of a man can achieve.

Napoleon Hill

#156 June 4

Your success as a sales person is not related to your ability to give information, but rather to your ability to get information.

#157 June 5

If you want customer loyalty, you must be loyal to the customer.

Regis Mckenna

#158 June 6

If you want to know what people want, ask them—and listen to what they have to say.

#159 June 7

Discipline yourself to do the things you need to do when you need to do them, and the day will come when you will be able to do the things you want to do when you want to do them.

Zig Ziglar

#160 June 8

A professional salesperson's most valuable asset is reputation. What are you doing to build yours?

#161 June 9

No one person can get very far in this life on a forty-hour week.

J.W. Marriott

#162 June 10

Sell your customers what they want, not what you "think" they need.

#163 June 11

Positioning: If you're standing second in line, in enough lines, sooner or later you're going to move up to number one.

#164 June 12

You can make yourself sick with your thoughts, and you can make yourself well with them. Negative thoughts create negative emotions that take energy out of you. Positive thoughts and images create positive emotions and restore your energy. Action creates motivation. Action is the best medicine I know.

#165 June 13

There are two common traits among all good salespeople: first, they love to make sales and of equal importance, they respect their customers.

#166 June 14

The best way to get people to believe in you is to believe in yourself.

#167 June 15

If you are a sales veteran, don't overlook learning from the rookies.

#168 June 16

Short thank you notes yield long results. Make them hand-written, hand-stamped, and mailed the same day as any sales call or meeting.

#169 June 17

Develop relationships with people at various decision-making levels within your accounts. Personnel changes are inevitable

#170 June 18

We are the CEO of our own business; therefore we must invest in ourselves.

#171 June 19

Be as critical of yourself as you are of others.

#172 June 20

Know the lifetime value of your prospects and customers.

#173 June 21

The sooner you realize how short life is, the quicker you'll write your own agenda.

#174 June 22

If you care at all, you'll get some results. If you care enough, you'll get incredible results.

#175 June 23

If you go to work on your goals, your goals will go to work on you. If you go to work on your plan, your plan will go to work on you. Whatever good things we build end up building us.

#176 June 24

Every single word the customer says has value.

Richard Mcginn

#177 June 25

They want to know what it will do, not what it is.

#178 June 26

To succeed in selling, use emotion and logic in your sales presentation. Logic makes people think. Emotion makes them act.

Zig Ziglar

#179 June 27

In sales, you get the customers you deserve. If you want to be a better salesperson, seek out better customers.

Mark H. Mccormack

#180 June 28

Don't be boring, at any time, in any way, when wearing the "sales hat."

#181 June 29

People buy from people that they like, often regardless of price.

#182 June 30

Be aggressive, not oppressive!

#183 July 1

What you find at the top of the mountain is what you brought there.

#184 July 2

Be sure to ask your satisfied customers for referrals. Ask for testimonial letters when you ask for referrals.

#185 July 3

You can't sell anybody anything . . . until they discover they want it.

#186 July 4

Radical technological change will continue through the rest of your career. If you don't cope with it, you will be left behind.

Thomas Siebel

#187 July 5

If you can differentiate a dead chicken, you can differentiate anything.

Frank Perdue

There is no such thing as a commodity. All goods and services are differentiable.

Ted Levitt

#188 July 6

When someone buys, they want to feel like they have something special. "People will buy anything that's one to a customer."

Sinclair Lewis

#189 July 7

We will get paid what we are worth, once we prove our worth.

#190 July 8

Your success as a salesperson is not related to your ability to give information, but rather to your ability to get information. ("One of the best ways to persuade others is with your ears—by listening to them.")

Dean Rusk

#191 July 9

If we all did the things we are capable of doing, we would literally astound ourselves.

Thomas Edison

#192 July 10

It is more important to reach the people who count, than to count the people you reach.

#193 July 11

Creating interest is a good way to prospect customers.

#194 July 12

The person who wants to do something finds a way; the person who doesn't finds an excuse.

#195 July 13

An unaspiring person believes according to what he achieves. An aspiring person achieves according to what he believes.

Sri Chinmoy

#196 July 14

A smart business person is one who makes a mistake, learns from it, and never makes it again. A wise business person is one who finds a smart business person and learns from him how to avoid the mistakes he made.

Jim Abrams

#197 July 15

To succeed, be daring, be first, be different.

#198 July 16

Ambition without initiative is simply day-dreaming.

#199 July 17

Nothing happens until someone sells something.

#200 July 18

A professional is one who does his best work when he feels the least like working.

Frank Lloyd Wright

#201 July 19

Often, you have to rely on intuition.

Bill Gates

#202 July 20

The most motivating thing one person can do for another is to listen.

Roy Moody

#203 July 21

When you fly by the seat of your pants, expect turbulence!

Vinit Saxena

#204 July 22

No mistake or failure is as bad as to stop and not try again.

John Wanamaker

#205 July 23

God gave us two ears but only one mouth. Some people say that's because he wanted us to spend twice as much time listening as talking. Others claim it's because he knew that listening was twice as hard. One who listens well tends to sell well.

#206 July 24

When economic times tighten, the sales professional will surface through valued relationships.

#207 July 25

If my competitors were drowning, I'd put a hose in their mouth.

Ray Kroc

#208 July 26

When the need is great enough, the expertise great enough, price is not a factor.

Max Carey

#209 July 27

Model the masters. Learn from the best.

#210 July 28

Treasure awaits—outside the dots. Be creative—it often results in higher margins, fewer crowds, and more fun.

Jack Daly

#211 July 29

You never get a second chance to make a first impression.

#212 July 30

Psychological Reciprocity: People will treat you the way you treat them.

#213 July 31

Your goal: To get many from a few instead of a few from many. Think share of customer, not market share.

#214 August 1

Never make a call without a purpose

#215 August 2

It is essential that we continually upgrade our clientele in order to increase our production.

#216 August 3

It isn't the quantity of calls that creates sales success; it's the quality of each call that counts.

#217 August 4

Just Stop:

- Stop talking so much on your calls.
- Stop giving up after the second call.
- Stop "dropping in" on important clients. Work by appointment.
- Stop worrying about the quantity of your calls.
- Stop making only the "comfort" calls.

#218 August 5

Remember—people care more about what's in your heart than what's in your head.

#219 August 6

Relationship selling is a productivity game, not a numbers game.

#220 August 7

Never make a presentation without handouts with your name on them.

#221 August 8

Dynamics of selling:

- Sales don't just happen
- 80% occur after the fifth call
- 48% of sales people make one call and quit
- 24% make two calls and quit
- 20% keep calling
- These are the 20% who do 80% of the business!

#222 August 9

There is no better way to let people know you are interested in them or care about them than to listen to them.

#223 August 10

If you're not adding value, you're subtracting it.

#224 August 11

Practice does not make perfect. Only perfect practice makes perfect.

#225 August 12

The progress of selling operates like a bank. Before making withdrawals you must first make deposits. Be sure you are dealing in your client's currency.

#226 August 13

It is better to wear out than rust out.

Richard Cumberland

#227 August 14

Remember that every bad situation could be worse—like the man who cursed his luck because he had no shoes, until he met a man who had no feet.

#228 August 15

The world makes way for the man who knows where he is going.

Ralph Waldo Emerson

#229 August 16

Your prospect's enthusiasm for your product or service is a product of your enthusiasm for your product or service.

#230 August 17

The secret to success is to do the common things uncommonly well.

John D. Rockerfeller Jr.

#231 August 18

The best way to learn to sell is to go out and sell. Trial and error are the two greatest sales instructors.

#232 August 19

The only two things people ever buy are good feelings and solutions to problems.

#233 August 20

What percentage of your customers total business are you receiving?

#234 August 21

I am the only one; but I am still one. I cannot do everything, but I can still do something. I will not refuse to do the something I can do.

Helen Keller

#235 August 22

Nothing in the world can take the place of persistence. Talent will not; nothing is more common than unsuccessful men with talent. Genius will not; unrewarded genius is almost a proverb. Education will not; the world is full of educated failures. Persistence and determination alone are omnipotent.

#236 August 23

As a salesperson, keeping track of your time is the moral equivalent of a dieter counting calories, except you're monitoring your output, not your intake.

#237 August 24

Rely on your support staff. Your time should be spent in front of the customer, not in the office.

#238 August 25

No salesperson ever listened themselves out of a sale.

#239 August 26

All customers should not be treated equally; some deserve more attention than others. Yet, for all, there is a base-line level of service. Treat them accordingly.

Jack Daly

#240 August 27

Goals. There's no telling what you can do when you get inspired by them. There's no telling what you can do when you believe in them. There's no telling what will happen when you act upon them.

#241 August 28

Motivation is a mystery. Why does one sales person see his first prospect at seven in the morning and another salesperson is just getting out of bed at eleven? I don't know. It's part of the mysteries of life.

#242 August 29

When the promise is clear, the price gets easy.

#243 August 30

Customers will find a way to buy from you if they like you. They will also find a way not to buy from you if they don't like you.

#244 August 31

You can get everything in life you want, if you help enough other people get what they want.

Zig Ziglar

#245 September 1

Look at each lead as a sales relationship—and remember that relationships take time to develop.

#246 September 2

Only a few objections come up with regularity. Why not prepare for them?

#247 September 3

The most productive day of the year is the same for all of us . . . . The day before vacation. Imagine each day being so organized and focused!

#248 September 4

When it comes to customers, what matters most isn't what you know or whom you know, but how you are known to them.

Michael Leboeuf

#249 September 5

One of the best things you can do for a wavering prospect is eliminate his fear. Propose a trial run.

#250 September 6

Nothing will improve a person's hearing more than sincere praise. Let your customers, as well as your company support team, know you appreciate them.

#251 September 7

Instead of talking about how valuable we are, we should learn how we can be of value.

David A. Peoples

#252 September 8

It's not whether you get knocked down. It's whether you get up again.

Vince Lombardi

#253 September 9

Ability is important—dependability is critical.

Zig Ziglar

#254 September 10

The greatest selling lesson comes down to this: never say no for the other guy.

Harvey Mackay

#255 September 11

The world is moving so fast these days that the man who says it can be done is generally interrupted by someone doing it.

Elbert Hubbard

#256 September 12

We don't need every customer, just the right customers.

#257 September 13

Opportunity is missed by most people because it is dressed in overalls and looks like work.

#258 September 14

I don't look to jump over 7-foot bars; I look around for 1-foot bars that I can step over.

Warren Buffet

(Seek the most direct route to solutions)

#259 September 15

Take your work seriously and yourself lightly.

Bob Nelson

#260 September 16

The clearer your definition of success, the greater your chances of reaching success. If you fail to define success, you can never hope to reach it.

#261 September 17

Set your goals high. People who expect more, get more.

Jack Kaine

#262 September 18

I never worry about action, only inaction.

Winston Churchhill

#263 September 19

Nothing is more rewarding than to watch someone who says it can't be done get interrupted by someone who is actually doing it.

#264 September 20

People are always blaming their circumstances. The people who get on in this world are the people who get up and look for the circumstances they want, and if they can't find them, they make them.

George Bernard Shaw

#265 September 21

We are what we think we are. Don't limit yourself . . . raise the bar.

#266 September 22

Customers will go out of their way to buy a superior product . . . and you can charge them a toll for the trip.

Frank Perdue

#267 September 23

Seek Failure. Unless you allow yourself to make mistakes, to fail, you will never have the opportunity to test the limits of what you are truly capable of accomplishing.

#268 September 24

People are different. Treat them accordingly.

#269 September 25

Never quote price until you have established value.

Jim Pratt

#270 September 26

People like to buy, not to be sold. A sales professional helps people to buy by providing value.

#271 September 27

Success leaves clues. Learn from other top-performing sales professionals.

#272 September 28

"What do I want them to remember when I'm gone?" Consider this before making a sales call and prepare accordingly.

#273 September 29

Goals not written are dreams. Dreams don't often come true. Goals in writing do.

Jack Daly

#274 September 30

Sources of business:

- New customers
- Existing customers
- Former customers

Have a plan to increase your share with each.

#275 October 1

Risk failure. To not risk it, ensures it.

#276 October 2

Objections are needs not met. Find the way to meet them.

#277 October 3

Success comes in a can, not in a can't. Develop a successful attitude.

#278 October 4

Competitive differentiation comes more from follow-up than from presentation.

#279 October 5

Maintain a client profile on each of your clients and prospects. Recognize it is never finished.

#280 October 6

Effective presenters practice:
- Tell 'em what you're going to tell 'em
- Tell 'em
- Tell 'em what you told 'em

#281 October 7

More sales calls equal more sales.

#282 October 8

Create and distribute a personal resume, detailing your particular unique background and capabilities. People do business with people. Represent yourself in the market as someone your prospects would like to do business with.

#283 October 9

The first two letters in the word "goal" are "go." Take action!

#284 October 10

If you aren't fired with enthusiasm, you will be fired with enthusiasm.

#285 October 11

The commissions you earn on the sales you almost make are the same in all industries.

#286 October 12

No one strives for mediocrity. But an awful lot of people settle for it. Go the extra mile, and positively differentiate yourself.

#287 October 13

Whenever you have contact with a customer, you are the company to that customer.

#288 October 14

We all need lots of powerful long-range goals to help us past the short-term obstacles.

#289 October 15

Do you add enough value to more than compensate for the difference in your competitors lower price?

#290 October 16

Listen to customers. They're quite willing to say what kind of service they want and to rate the service they're getting.

#291 October 17

Touch your prospects, customers and clients on an ongoing basis. These "touches" should go beyond you and your products. Touch them with ideas to help them grow their business.

Jack Daly

#292 October 18

A whisper from a happy client is louder than a salesperson.

#293 October 19

We can no more afford to spend major time on minor things than we can to spend minor time on major things.

#294 October 20

If you are not willing to risk the unusual, you will have to settle for the ordinary.

#295 October 21

Thinking is easy. Action is difficult.

#296 October 22

People buy for one reason only, for emotional satisfaction, and the more immediate the gratification, the faster they will buy.

#297 October 23

They are thinking about buying when they ask the price. Be prepared with benefits valued by the prospect.

#298 October 24

People buy emotionally and justify with logic. Use both logic and emotion to win and keep customers.

#299 October 25

Keep your name on the minds of your prospects so when the door of opportunity opens, you are the first one in line.

C. Richard Weylman

#300 October 26

Selling is the transfer of trust.

#301 October 27

Questions, interest and knowledge are the building blocks of a business partnership.

#302 October 28

Individuals and organizations that are good react quickly to change. Individuals and organizations that are great create change. Anticipate, don't react. Change before you have to.

Robert Kriegel

#303 October 29

Future sales can be increased by properly taking care of today's customers.

#304 October 30

I've always made a total effort, even when the odds seemed entirely against me. I never quit trying; I never felt that I didn't have a chance to win.

Arnold Palmer

#305 October 31

A mediocre salesperson tells. A good salesperson explains. A superior salesperson demonstrates. A great salesperson inspires the buyers to see the benefits as their own.

#306 November 1

Two shoe salesmen . . . find themselves in a rustic backward part of Africa. The first salesman wires back to his head office: "There is no prospect of sales, natives do not wear shoes!" The other salesman wires: "No one wears shoes here. We can dominate the market. Send all the possible stock." (Check your attitude!)

#307 November 2

You miss 100 percent of the shots you never take.

Wayne Gretzky

#308 November 3

People will trust their eyes far before they will ever trust your words.

Harry Beckwith

#309 November 4

You can close more business in two months by becoming interested in other people than you can in two years by trying to get people interested in you.

Dale Carnegie

#310 November 5

Every single person you meet has a sign around his or her neck that says, "make me feel important." If you can do that, you'll be a success not only in business but in life too.

Mary Kay Ash

#311 November 6

The one person who's always happy to teach you a lesson is a tough competitor. Learn to benchmark from the best.

#312 November 7

There are two things people want more than sex and money . . . Recognition and praise.

Mary Kay Ash

#313 November 8

If you don't know where you are going, you will probably end up somewhere else.

Laurence J. Peter

#314 November 9

Practice the Platinum Rule: Do unto others . . . the way they want to be done unto.

#315 November 10

To get to the top of the sales profession, you've got to practice, practice, and practice. Find a system that works, and learn it, spend enough time getting to know it, and soon you will own it.

David H. Sandler

#316 November 11

What is the most valuable use of my time—now? Discover the answer, and do it.

#317 November 12

When you talk, you only learn what you already know.

#318 November 13

Making each day count is a tactic. Making each year count is a strategy. You need both to succeed.

Harvey Mackay

#319 November 14

Build a database of previous clients, current clients and prospective clients and design a program of regular communication with each.

#320 November 15

When you're through changing, you're through.

Bruce Barton

#321 November 16

He who asks questions cannot avoid the answers.

Cameroon Proverb

#322 November 17

Enjoy the power of positioning. Maintain ongoing contact with targeted prospects.

#323 November 18

Execute Passionately. Marginal tactics executed passionately almost always will outperform brilliant tactics executed marginally.

Harry Beckwith

#324 November 19

Do not let what you cannot do interfere with what you can do.

Steve Wooden

#325 November 20

You can have brilliant ideas, but if you can't get them across, your ideas won't get you anywhere.

Lee Iacocca

#326 November 21

Compensation is a right. Recognition is a gift.

Rosabeth Moss Kanter

#327 November 22

Ask your customers for referrals.

#328 November 23

Efficiency: doing things right
Effectiveness: doing right things
Excellence: doing right things right

#329 November 24

Two questions worth asking yourself <u>before</u> making any sales call:

• What is the purpose of this call?
• What kind of person am I calling on?

#330 November 25

Two questions worth asking yourself immediately <u>following</u> any sales call:

- Did I achieve the purpose of the call?
- What kind of person did I call on?

#331 November 26

If there's not much difference between your product or service and that of your competition, then there had better be a big difference in the way you deal with people.

David A. Peoples

#332 November 27

It is no use saying, "We are doing our best." You have to succeed in doing what is necessary.

Winston Churchill

#333 November 28

When it comes to customers, what matters most isn't what you know or whom you know, but how you are known to them.

#334 November 29

Sell only what you are sold on. If you don't believe in your product or your company, don't sell it.

#335 November 30

Position and differentiate your company with a unique selling proposition. It tells the customer exactly what makes you special enough to want to do business with you and not your competitor.

James P. Cecil

#336 December 1

In the factory we make cosmetics, but in my store we sell hope.

Charles Revlon, Founder-Revlon Cosmetics

(What are you selling?)

#337 December 2

You'll never learn what your customers want if you are too busy watching what your competitors are doing.

Thomas Winninger

#338 December 3

The way to do more with less is to do less. Be clear on what will have the greatest impact on your goals and focus your efforts primarily on doing those things well.

Bob Nelson

#339 December 4

My job is to get people to do what they don't want to do, so they can be what they've always wanted to be.

Tom Landry

#340 December 5

Definiteness of purpose is the starting point of all achievement.

W. Clement Stone

#341 December 6

Even if you're on the right track you'll get run over if you just sit there.

Will Rogers

#342 December 7

Think of objections as the details that need to be worked out, and be prepared before the sales call.

#343 December 8

Before deciding whether to buy, the prospect asks himself two questions:
1. Why do business with you? Develop a show-stopping response.
2. Why do business with your company? Make your response irresistible to your prospect.

#344 December 9

The primary reason your customer does not buy is his or her fear of making a bad decision.

#345 December 10

The sale is a courtship. How good the marriage is depends on how well the seller maintains the relationship.

#346 December 11

When you are selling an interview put the emphasis on getting the prospect to agree to a meeting, not on the merits of your product.

#347 December 12

When you eliminate excuses, you get rid of all the other problems. When you get rid of the other problems, you will make room for the positives. When you make room for the positives, you get results.

#348 December 13

If you can dream it you can do it.

Walt Disney

#349 December 14

Share success with the people who make it happen. It makes everybody think like an owner, which helps them build long-term relationships with customers and influences them to do things in an efficient way.

Emily Ericsen

#350 December 15

Nobody wants your product. Nobody wants your service. They only want what your product or service will do for them now.

Chuck Reaves

#351 December 16

A professional is someone who can do his best work when he doesn't feel like it.

Alistar Cooke

#352 December 17

Your business should be market driven—not product driven.

#353 December 18

The best way to minimize objections is to define the highest value needs and meet them.

#354 December 19

Positioning—Be a consistent and strong number two with each of your target prospect accounts.

#355 December 20

Send birthday and anniversary cards.

#356 December 21

The professional salesperson is a facilitator, not a pitchman.

#357 December 22

Understand your differentiation from others. Then, use those skills whenever you have the opportunity.

#358 December 23

People will teach you how to sell them if you'll pay attention to the messages they send you.

#359 December 24

In business, the competition will bite you if you keep running; if you stand still, they will swallow you.

William S. Knudsen

#360 December 25

Always have several written testimonials, dated within 90 days, ready for distribution.

#361 December 26

Judge your ability to give a good sales presentation by your ability to listen. You'll see more by listening than by talking.

#362 December 27

Lead with need, and not with product.

#363 December 28

Successful people always have a carrot in front of them, slightly out of reach, no matter how many carrots they already have.

#364 December 29

If you listen closely enough, your customers will explain your business to you.

Peter Schutz

#365 December 30

Do what you say you're going to do, the way you say you're going to do it, when you say you're going to do it.

#366 December 31

If you have to swallow a frog—don't sit down and look at it very long. If you have to eat several, eat the biggest one first.

About the Author
Jack Daly

Jack Daly brings 20 plus years of field proven experience—from a starting base with the CPA firm of Arthur Andersen to the CEO level of several national companies. Jack has participated at the senior executive level on four de novo businesses, two of which were subsequently sold to the Wall Street firms of Solomon Brothers and First Boston.

As the head of sales and production, Jack has led sales forces numbering in the thousands, operating out of hundreds of offices nationwide. His leadership experience was shaped at the Fleet Mortgage Group, Security Pacific Bank, Glenfed Mortgage Corporation, Home Mortgage Access Corporation and Evans Products Corporation.

A few highlights include:

➢ Headed sales for America's 4th largest national mortgage banker, as well as the $15 billion California division of the nation's 5th largest savings bank.

➢ In 1985 relocated from the East Coast to California to lead a mortgage company start-up. As CEO, Jack spurred growth to

22 branches operating in 40 states, with 750 employees, generating $350 million per month in mortgages. Over the initial 3 year period, reported earnings of $42 million.

Jack was born and raised in Philadelphia, Pennsylvania, and currently resides in San Juan Capistrano, California. Jack's education includes an MBA from Wilmington College, a BS from LaSalle University, and the rank of Captain in the U.S. Army.

Jack currently wears two hats: COO (Chief Opportunity Officer) of Platinum Capital Group, and CEO (Chief Energizing Officer) of Professional Sales Coach, Inc.

PLATINUM CAPITAL GROUP

Platinum Capital Group operates as a full-service national mortgage company, headquartered in Southern California. The eight-year old privately held company garnered significant recognition in 1998 as a fast growth/high performance industry leader, to include: Ernst & Young Entrepreneur of the Year; Top Ten on the Inc. 500; Blue Chip Enterprise Award from the U.S. Chamber of Commerce; and ranked #1 Fastest Growing Privately Held Company in Los Angeles.

17101 Armstrong Avenue
Suite 200, Irvine, CA 92614
(949) 221-0800
www.PlatinumCapital.com

Professional Sales Coach, Inc.

Professional Sales Coach, Inc. (PSC), is a sales and sales leadership training and consulting firm. PSC's core business is coaching companies to greater sales and profits. As a result of demand world-wide, Jack Daly delivers keynote presentations for industry conferences and company sales and customer events.

Jack's custom-designed programs deliver results. On several occasions Jack has spoken to YEO Universities and Inc. Magazine conferences, garnering highest rated speaker honors.

Professional Sales Coach's cutting difference is "speaking from experience."

Professional Sales Coach
23 Calle Pacifica
San Clemente, CA 92673

Professional Sales Coach Training Tools by Jack Daly

		With Work Book	Without Work Book *(Please circle your selection in these columns)*	Quantity
Building A World Class Sales Organization (Sales Management - Live - 3 hours)	A) Video	$150	N/A	
	B) Audio Cassette	$40	$30	
	C) CD	$50	$40	
Smart Selling Through Value (Sales Training - Live - 3 hours)	D) Video	$150	N/A	
	E) Audio Cassette	$40	$30	
	F) CD	$50	$40	
Relationship Selling (Sales Training - Studio Recorded - 6 hours)	G) Audio Cassette	$75	N/A	
Achieving Leadership Excellence (Sales Management - Studio Recorded - 6 hours)	H) Audio Cassette	$75	N/A	
Books etc	Daly Sales Motivators (Book)	N/A	$15	
	Daly Sales Motivators (Perpetual Calendar)	N/A	$15	
	Building A World Class Sales Organization	N/A	$15	
	Smart Selling	N/A	$15	
	Marketing Magic	N/A	$15	
Package Specials	** Videos "A" + "D"	$250	N/A	
	** Audios "B" + "E"	$70	$50	
	** CD's "C" + "F"	$80	$60	

** Less 10% Discount on orders over $250.00 **   **SUB-TOTAL:** _____

Applicable California sales tax, shipping & handling will be added to invoice.   **TOTAL PURCHASE AMOUNT:** _____

PLEASE FILL OUT THE PAYMENT OPTIONS AND SHIPPING INFORMATION ON THE BACK SIDE OF THIS FORM

For product information or speaking inquiries, please contact:

Jack Daly

Professional Sales Coach, Inc.
23 Calle Pacifica
San Clemente, CA 92673

Telephone: (888) 298-6868
Fax: (866) 870-0546
www.ProfessionalSalesCoach.net

TOTAL AMOUNT OF PURCHASE

$ _____

☐ **Yes!** *Please add my name to your distribution list for a free Email Sales Management Newsletter.*

Name _____ Date _____

Company _____

Street Address _____

City _____ State _____ Zip _____

Day Phone _____ Email _____

☐ VISA
☐ MC   Card No. ___/___/___/___/___/___/___/___/___/___/___/___/
☐ AMEX

Exp. date ____ / ____   Signature _____

VISA®

MasterCard®

AMERICAN EXPRESS